Machines with Power!

Dump Trucks

by Amy McDonald

BLASTOFF! Beginners

BELLWETHER MEDIA
MINNEAPOLIS, MN

Blastoff! Beginners are developed by literacy experts and educators to meet the needs of early readers. These engaging informational texts support young children as they begin reading about their world. Through simple language and high frequency words paired with crisp, colorful photos, Blastoff! Beginners launch young readers into the universe of independent reading.

Sight Words in This Book 🔍

a	for	it	out	this
are	go	look	the	to
at	help	make	these	
big	is	one	they	

This edition first published in 2021 by Bellwether Media, Inc.

No part of this publication may be reproduced in whole or in part without written permission of the publisher. For information regarding permission, write to Bellwether Media, Inc., Attention: Permissions Department, 6012 Blue Circle Drive, Minnetonka, MN 55343.

Library of Congress Cataloging-in-Publication Data

Names: McDonald, Amy, 1985- author.
Title: Dump trucks / by Amy McDonald.
Description: Minneapolis, MN : Bellwether Media, Inc. 2021. | Series: Blastoff! Beginners : Machines with power! | Includes bibliographical references and index. | Audience: Ages PreK-2 | Audience: Grades K-1 |
Identifiers: LCCN 2020029228 (print) | LCCN 2020029229 (ebook) | ISBN 9781644873694 (library binding) | ISBN 9781648340703 (ebook)
Subjects: LCSH: Dump trucks--Juvenile literature.
Classification: LCC TL230.15 .M427 2021 (print) | LCC TL230.15 (ebook) | DDC 629.225--dc23
LC record available at https://lccn.loc.gov/2020029228
LC ebook record available at https://lccn.loc.gov/2020029229

Editor: Christina Leaf   Designer: Andrea Schneider

Printed in the United States of America, North Mankato, MN.

Table of Contents

What Are Dump Trucks?

Beep! Beep!
A dump truck is
at the job site!

Dump trucks are strong machines. They carry big **loads**.

load

Parts of a Dump Truck

This is the **engine**. It makes the dump truck go.

engine

These are
the wheels.
They help the
truck move.

wheels

This is the **cab**.
It is for the driver.

cab

This is the **dump box**. It holds the load.

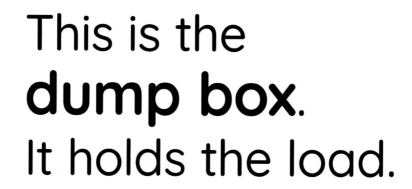

dump box

Dump Trucks at Work

This dump truck
moves snow.
The road is clear!

This one is full.
It brings sand
to a job site.

This one
dumps rocks.
Look out!

Dump Truck Facts

p Truck Parts

cab

dump box

wheel

Glossary

cab

a place for the driver

dump box

the part of a dump truck that carries the load

engine

the part of a dump truck that makes it go

loads

what dump trucks carry

To Learn More

ON THE WEB

FACTSURFER

Factsurfer.com gives you a safe, fun way to find more information.

1. Go to www.factsurfer.com.

2. Enter "dump trucks" into the search box and click 🔍.

3. Select your book cover to see a list of related content.

Index

The images in this book are reproduced through the courtesy of: Art Konovalov, front cover, p. 3; Bogdan Mircea Hoda, pp. 4-5; seroma72, pp. 6-7; Tom Cassidy/ Alamy, pp. 8-9, 23 (engine); Image by Ronald Plett from Pizabay, pp. 10-11; Samuel Acosta, pp. 12 (cab), 22 (parts); RosaIreneBetancourt 10/ Alamy, pp. 12-13; 2windspa, pp. 14 (dump box), 23 (cab); wbritten, pp. 14-15; nikitos77, pp. 16-17, 22 (move snow); kasoga, pp. 18-19; Debove Sophie, pp. 20-21; TFoxFoto, p. 22 (load to site); Iron_Man_, p. 22 (dump); DarthArt, p. 23 (dump box); PetraMeclovaCZ, p. 23 (loads).